The Firetalker's Daughter

poems by

Regina YC Garcia

Finishing Line Press
Georgetown, Kentucky

The Firetalker's Daughter

Copyright © 2023 by Regina YC Garcia
ISBN 979-8-88838-188-5 First Edition
All rights reserved under International and Pan-American Copyright Conventions. No part of this book may be reproduced in any manner whatsoever without written permission from the publisher, except in the case of brief quotations embodied in critical articles and reviews.

ACKNOWLEDGMENTS

I am the daughter and the mother of Firetalkers, so these musings are in some parts autobiographical, yet in every part, real.

Previously Published and Forthcoming Poetry Contained in *The FireTalker's Daughter*

*Garcia, Regina YC. "Deeper...Further...Back." Edited by Marlen Harrison, *The AutoEthnographer—A LITERARY & ARTS MAGAZINE*, Nov. 2022, https://theautoethnographer.com/.
Garcia, Regina YC. "Sonnet 1: Black Girl from Night to Light." Edited by Ruchi Acharya, *Book of Black*, Wingless Dreamer, 25 Oct. 2021.
Garcia, Regina YC. "The Fire Consumes: The Burnings of Black Histories." *SoFloPoJo*, Aug. 2021, https://www.southfloridapoetryjournal.com/sfpj-video.html.
Garcia, Regina YC. "Voice." *Black And...*, Sapphire Hues, 2021, http://sapphirehues.com/black-and-issue-1/.
Garcia, Regina YC. "This Fire Tastes Like." *Backstory of the Poem* #401, 2023, https://chrisricecooper.com/401-backstory-of-the-poem-this-fire-tastes-like-from-the-poetry-collection-the-firetalkers-daughter-by-regina-yc-garcia/.

Publisher: Leah Huete de Maines
Editor: Christen Kincaid
Cover Art: Camryn Harrell
Author Photo: Regina YC Garcia
Cover Design: Elizabeth Maines McCleavy

Order online: www.finishinglinepress.com
also available on amazon.com

Author inquiries and mail orders:
Finishing Line Press
PO Box 1626
Georgetown, Kentucky 40324
USA

Table of Contents

The Firetalker's Daughter 1

Sonnet 1: Black Girl-From Night to Light................................2

My Shrines...3

On Mountains and Mothers...4

from The Book Found in the Rubble 5

The Fire That Consumes: The Burnings of Black Histories 6

Voice..8

I Call Fire..10

They have taken nothing 11

Hallowed Grounds: Sacred Sites of African American Memory 13

Afro Futures: Rest Stops 14

The Air Bears Witness..16

Way Brown Belle..19

Salt? 21

die no more 23

Creeks..24

Deeper…Further…Back...26

If you want this strength..28

The Fire Tastes Like…..30

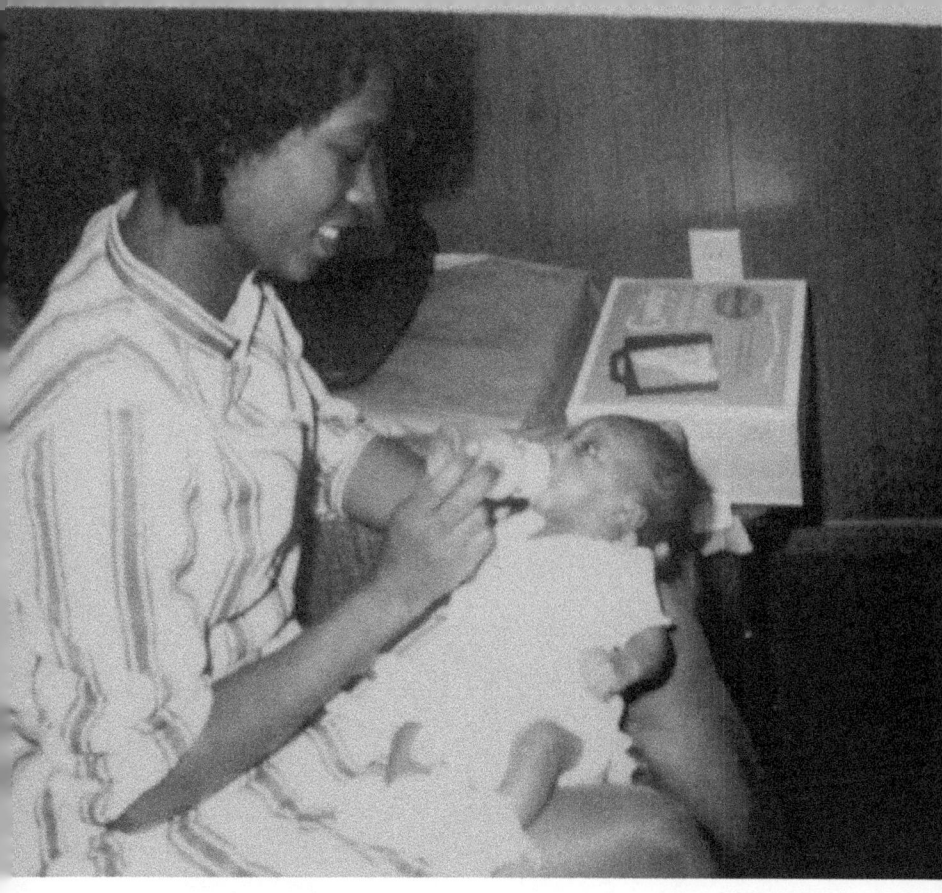

This book is an homage of love to my mother, Evelyn Simpson Carter, a Firetalker from a line of great healers who have born that tortuous pain away from those afflicted in mind, body, and spirit.

These words that follow reflect of the both edifying and destructive nature of the fires that burn within us and around us.

The Firetalker's Daughter

My mother "talked the fire" out of burns, eased the pain, as did her father, as did his mother as does my son, as will his daughter…
It had to pass me by, as I was not a man child
Yet my mother looked at me like I was sun in the sky… like I was promise
She said that while I would not have that gift, I would have a great many, and even though I couldn't "talk it," I most certainly carried it
Power
I entered the world, very tiny and gray with a gray ring around my brown eyes—Said I was "scrawny" with bright eyes that had "seen before"
Mama said a great many long-gone spirits dwelled where I was born, and when it was time to leave that place, she was well ready to go. They worried her incessantly
She told me many other things like how Great Aunties "Hat" and "At" were healers, and women would come to them for many an unknown ailment and how God put these abilities in us because of what God knew we would need to survive
For our families to survive
For our people to survive
My mother marched in "the movement"
My mother educated the masses
My mother spoke the Fire
But sometimes, my mother held her tongue
My mother can no longer tell me anymore about these truths I have discovered are very real—That is to say that she lives, but she cannot say
Sometimes her tongue gets confused. Sometimes her tongue is at rest.
I cannot talk the fire
Yet, I am Fire
I know this because she told me so
Truth

Sonnet 1: Black Girl-From Night to Light

Bereft in dark, tongue-bound, can hardly speak
Birthed into black light stations me a witch
For tis my trial to bear my burdens weak
While World adjusts my heart song to its pitch

While I can neither peel nor walk away
From skin that scorches bronze within sun's glare
My mother carries spells throughout her day
And keeps her daughter in her careful stare
For who am I to battle sin-sick souls,
Who raise their swords to slice my words from me?
My ancient magic renders demons cold
A thought that surely sets my spirit free

As much as I now know, I must give flame,
And now that I am here, I must remain.

My Shrines

I build shrines with hot and angry tears; the most holy are these I have shed
These are the ones that bigots mock, yet the ones that they most dread I
grow dark flowers in twisting pain, birthed in the narrows of my throat
Strewn across my fiery altars, they smell of dwindling hope
I light candles in my heart, to warm from rising chill

I kneel in desperation, pray these evil spirits still

I place symbols of the martyred, now in ancestral lands
I pray their sacrifice inhabit and solidify our stand
I call True God to impart the plan that will pointedly define
My role in this revolution to ease my troubled mind

On Mountains and Mothers

I have birthed mountains...
That tower beyond the highest peaks, formed within me, stretched in front of me, now steadily trying to overgrow my reach

I have birthed mountains...
And I ask that though they not stay, that their chosen way move them higher, closer, clearly, not over, but nearly to the places that bless them the most
Surrounded by hosts that usher them into the presence of the primer and polisher of perfection, humbler of their boast

Oh, I've birthed strong mountains...
Their very best striations not made by me, but layered with stones of purpose and gifting by hands I could not see
My own eyes coated by the clay film marking my own humanity
Yet yes, I am blessed to bring forth a semblance of divinity, velveted, framed
Indeed, I have been ordained to love another trinity
that adds to the harmony
in lands and lives, maybe not yet seen nor conceived, not even by me.

I have birthed mountains...
Tripled peaks of promise so intriguing that I can barely entertain the meaning of how and why they burst into my life and turned my heart over and over and over
I can hardly contain the confining love that roars like fire to keep them in my grasp For them, I will blow fires that will incinerate their most vicious enemies
Keep away these horrors, Lord, for the prospect of their demise changes me
Alas, assignments shift and change and pass...

I have birthed mountains...
I've been the vessel and the maiden who poured
She who yet adores
them, who point and stretch toward the sky
She, who tries to drink back the selfish cry
As she continues to try
to remember that although their ascent is their own
Her prayers rendered will never leave them alone...

I have birthed mountains
Mighty, Mighty Mountains

from The Book Found in the Rubble

...and they kept watching in disbelief
shaking their heads/ waving their fingers/ promoting their angry twisted version of "God" until they were too spent to do what it took to destroy the weapon
designed to reform their expectations and excise a once progressive identity

...so accustomed to the language
to the diminish of human rights
to the world isolation
to the increase of weaponization
to the decrease of enrichment and access
to the disparate values assigned to human life
based on the most inalterable traits...
indeed, they were so numbed, that in the end
they barely felt the prick
or heard the click
or felt the searing of the fire that burned them through

...collective indoctrination, however, marked the entrance of a period of insidious desperation and distrust
created dramatic societal divide
halted the level of cooperation required to maintain and flourish

Every area of life became distinctively and disturbingly different

I scribble this with bloodied fingers.
It will likely be found in the age after we failed to address this great fire that tore through our land...
...you know...unless...

The Fire That Consumes: The Burnings of Black Histories

Have you ever seen fire, the kind that consumes...?
a house, a block, a street?
a community?
a town?
a nation?

Have you ever stretched fingers towards fire just because you wanted to feel the last gusts of breath before the flames melted...?
Mortar from brick?
Wood from steel?
Skin from meat from sinew from bone?
Have you ever jumped at the crack and splinter before the crash?
Hid your face to escape the blowing soot?
Covered your nose to block the smell of escaping gasses the incineration of flesh? Squeezed eyes shut to restrain the release of tears?

Fire destroys completely
Everything
Except memory
Those who have lived through fire never forget that all that was lost cannot be returned, cannot be restored
Pre-fire life flickering in memory

Have you ever known the indignity of stolen memory?
Of erasure of thought?
A disallowing of necessary history passed on from mind to mind
No collective storage
Trashed as disposable waste
Scores of nations and families of people relegated to one layer of life lived while other layers burned away
Withdrawn from the light of day
Layers that could have lit
the illumination of minds
the awareness of conditions

the recognition of irreverence and unrighteousness
the tackling of generational traumas
the overcoming of fear
the pride of resilience

Layers of heated memory
Deemed villainous
Tossed into the ashes
By thieves, those who dread
The power that it brings
And the rise of indomitable spirits from the embers

Voice

I have screamed for
An eternity
And sometimes it has been
Powerful
and
Terrible
It has moved the danger away
I have raised my torch and dared anybody to
Silence me
I have bared pointed teeth
Saliva pouring down my chin
Eyes bulging
Feet ready to run and jump and kick
I am the sound
I am the rage
Yet sometimes
I am tired
Frightened
No
Deathly afraid
I have called upon my mother spirits
Those assigned to me
to hold back the devils that have come
For me
Come for my children
(The greatest sources of my fear-
feeling the wind and wave of their hands
as they dodge my grasp)
My old woman spirit guides have heard my entreaty and
arrived, pocketbook handles
In the crooks of their arms
They've sung holy war songs and
Done ring dance and
Lit fires to purge my fear and
Sacrificed it on the altar of womanhood

No room for it (fear) in Blackness
No room for it (fear) in woman-ness
What a tragic combination of expectations
For a time

I thought I could fear without fear
Turns out that I cannot have those moments
Got to put on my good black woman

Grease her down
Smother her in high blood pressure
Cook her down in bad cholesterol
Band her like a tumor
And stand like it's no matter
Yet, I am matter
I am water
I am blood
I am bone
I am skin
I am eyes
I am limbs
I am lungs
I am ears
I am heart
I am weeping doubt
I am Fire
My tough old women
don't care
Better crazy
Than crying
My old woman spirits
Have told me that
I must 'be strong'
(That's what the stars told them)
They have lived it
They know
No pallets to rest
The charges given me

I Call Fire
A Call and Response

I call Fire!
Fire!
Shut up in my bones
I call Fire!
Fire!
Shut up in my bones
I call Fire!
Fire!
Shut up in my bones
To take this pain from me
I say Come now!
Come now!
Tell me what to do
I say Come now!
Come now!
Tell me what to do
I say Come now!
Come now!
Tell me what to do
To set my spirit free!
Flame say Loose me!
Loose me!
I know what to do
Flame say Loose me!
Loose me!

I know what to do
Flame say Loose me!
Loose me!
I know what to do
To heal this troubled land
You hold it in your hand
To heal this troubled land

They have taken nothing

They have taken nothing
The inconvenient who interfere
Mind-bound to oppress
Not your skin, your smile, your hair, your bones, your heart, your beauty,
nothing, despite the ripping, tearing, gnashing
For you will be blessed, anointed, reassembled in this land
and new lands

They have taken nothing
Not your mind, not your essence
Not your gifts
Not that which is seeded in you
Not that fire spirit that finds rest in your belly
Not that blackbird that sings the song in your soul

They have taken nothing
The fields in which your thoughts walk
The suns that even your closed eyes see
The waters under which you swim
over which you glide
Unfettered by monsters, minstrels
mistrials
The Ancestors guide you
The Creator made you
God born saves you
Spirit covers and reveals you
and reveals to you

They have taken nothing
They have tricks with no power
Shifting lights with no illumination
Hidden hands
Weak grasp
No understanding of your station
They have taken nothing
Only closed doors
Piteous attempts at control
For your amulets are scattered strategically
around the realm
around the world

Possessive earthen carnality is futile
They have taken nothing
For you are here, holding the keys
to every possession
and unrealized obsession that you have
that you are meant to have
Your riches stored
Your then, now, and to be
live in readiness
They have taken nothing
You still
Have
Everything

Hallowed Grounds: Sacred Sites of African American Memory

In my mind, there are sacred sites...
Striding and struggling
Striations of strain and strength...
in memories I once lived and those I inherited
I marvel at how they and I "made it over" as if we floated in on the broken
but braced backs of a superhuman ancestral brood
Perhaps fire-baptized for a time such as this

For how on earth, Heaven, or hell...
Dare I moved clay lips to laugh, lie, cry, love, preen, protest, speak and write
life, and dodge death?

Lord, I realize...
These sanctified places of terror, trial, and triumph are ordered in my
thoughts, a reminder that true freedom is always bought with a price of
great sacrifice and justified only through an
ointment of redemption

So, the Spirit moved...
among these places
Buried a flaming message in my forebearers, even while they were moaning
in manacles
Hallowed be thy name
Inspired their holy dance while in deprivation
Hallowed be thy name
Anticipated the Gilded Grace that would carry them
Hallowed be thy name
Praised The Divine for answered prayers whispered only in their thoughts...
Hallowed be thy name
in wholly fickle lands

Afro Futures: Rest Stops

I see my great granddaughter
Born beyond my eyes
Exuding a powerful necessary strength
Seeded generations before
Intermittently emerging
As my mothers and fathers followed stars and found rest along the way
Places never seen before opened to them
Hid them
Protected them
Taught them
Rest and direction
These gifts appeared-then

Now, in this revolution
Her ancestors fight the monsters
That were always there, yet
Suddenly, very seen

These beasts roam
Pointy knees, gritted teeth, foul cracked spirits
Preying on vulnerable Brown Skins
In streets
Homes
Sofas
Beds
Awake
Asleep
Laughing
Crying
Begging
Mama! Mama!
Alive
Then not

Beasts walk with
Privilege and power
Embedded everywhere
Donning human faces
Blending into communities
Pretending legitimate enlightened humanity
Interlopers driven

Looking for a way in
Again, inspiring a worldly insanity
Seeking to drive wedges between
What could be love…

Disease, Violence, and Terroristic Fire
Wage war in light, twilight, and midnight hours
Play out the ideation of Manifest Destiny
Sanctioned by systems never built for those with access to ancient souls who look like me

Pandemics-multiple-named and unnamed-rage
And urging from deep within demands release and permission to address these sins as bronzed bodies fall from lack of direction and rest.
No direction without rest

In the days of my human eyes, this is what I've seen

Yet, in my visions
Hidden spaces form in places where
The wise meet the weak
Find love, water, healing, food to eat
Understanding, teaching, and access to the ancient gifts
Learn how to wield them, learn how to live

These rest stops appear
In the before time of far tomorrows
I pray that I will see them before I die
These dens of direction and rest
That I might sit with my great granddaughter's hand in mine

Repaired
Recreated
Alive
Safe
Divine

The Air Bears Witness

Air
>Shaped breath of Divinity
>Fuel of humanity
>A silent sentient ambassador

Indeed
>Utterance
>Mobility
>Laughter
>Love
>All require...

Air
>Ever present
>Sustainer of life

Respect due
>Respect due

And yet on these todays
>Yea, even from the beginnings of days
>Air bears ugly witness
>To the first whispers of dishonored death

Death signaled by
>Raised brows
>Tears
>Anger
>Fears
>Agitated spirits
>That tell darkened depraved minds
>That there is indeed no other way

Air stares soundlessly
>As thoughts break through cracked lips
>Words traveling on its currents
>Into ears of waiting co-conspirators
>Or simply float
>Then sink back into skin
>To settle and harden in the minds that conceived it

    And the hearts that believe that Breath Disrupted
    Is the only way
    To take control of these uncertain times

Air is obliged
    To be pulled in and out of lungs
    Irrespective
    Of the evil
    Of the good

Air is there shifting uneasily
    When the brute punches straight through her face and breaks her teeth
    Blood pouring from the spaces
    Underneath, indiscreet

Air is there wildly uncomfortable
    When insanity, profanity, corruption, brutality
    Meet in alleyways and leave mothers
    Planning and digging graves

Air is there when the clamoring mob says
    "Let's catch one unaware"
    And Air conspires with Fire and watches as they bring the rope and tie it tightly on wearied feet that have tried to run
    Dragging life down dark roads
    In pop-up sundown towns

Air sees tracks of blood relentlessly
    Circle this place
    From age to age
    Circle this place

Air sees it all
    Trapped in even
    The most unholy
    The most undignified
        Rooms
        Makeshift tombs

While Bright Air's charge is to sustain
        The flesh in this domain
        Man's refrains
        Of violence and misery
        Savagely redirect its mission

And Air remains
        To give testimony
        Eternal testimony

For Air is divinely compelled
        Righteously compelled
        To stoically bear witness
        To it all

Way Brown Belle

Way Brown Belle
Young and southern born
Unbound mind and matter
Grew strong
Flowed and shaped
Into systems
That tightened and bound
Maligned

Way Brown Belle
Feigns unbothered
Brain having been
pressed towards
intellect prescribed
Power decides
when to see her
when not

Way Brown Belle
strives to slay
invisibility
fights Butterflies, Age and

Rage that find their way
into work
Yet another layer of angry fire
that she must carry
and piece out in diverse parcels
of respectability
so that closing ears might hear

Way Brown Belle
Weighs her dreams
against her time
Wonders when either
will dissolve
and leave one to speak
for the other
as their journey has kept the
space that exists between them
inconsistent and worrisome

Way Brown Belle
Still looks for her wings
that flames have kept from materializing
because the fiery flickers want her to stay
without resistance

Way Brown Belle
Remembers a time
when the Brown words around her
on pages and in mouths
emerged from a furious furnace
and lighted her soul
Sometimes now, they burn her heart

Way Brown Belle
Wants to write light
but now is not the time
Still, Fire

Salt?

Son of God
God fleshborn
says
"Ye are the salt…"[1]
We are the salt
Yet many "we"
Be syrupy
Be fakely free
Covertly weak, unsure
Overtly wandering
Claiming lands
Binding hands
Locking Ankles
Swearing Love
Diluting Love
Killing Love
Love is NOT them *(points out)*
Love is them *(points around)*
Love is me *(points to self)*
God is Him *(points up)*
God is Me *(thinks silently)*
Ain't no God in she
Ain't no God in He
Ain't no God in THEM
(Points around)
God in ME *(points to self)*
Dead water, preaching dread
Loving words, unloving lives
Be blindly following
Be ignorantly building
Manipulations
Machinations
Death
Celebrating
Unfreedom

---

[1] *"Matthew 5:13-16 KJV - Ye Are the Salt of the Earth: But If - Bible Gateway." Bible Gateway,* https://www.biblegateway.com/passage/?search=Matthew%205%3A13-16&version=KJV. *Accessed 26 July 2021.*

Missing irony
Boxing "in the name of God"
Absurdly "boxing God"
Cracked Earth boxing God...
Enslaved thought
T-shirt bought
Self-labeled
"Salt"
Yet
Watering down
Tilling perverse ground
Small gods
Broken gods
Breaking lives
Enraged and enraptured with knees in protest
Cheering those knees kneeling
as instruments
Of death
Wrecking and rewriting
Truths of pain, fame, glory, destruction
Self-Idealized salt
Carrying vaults of self-righteous fury
Home to a God of their own creation
While True God, in all names, spirits,
and manifestations, continues to inspire
Divine Flavor

die no more
> *A Requiem for Breonna Taylor*

I take her up in my arms
A daughter I never knew
Daughter, die no more
Spirit ushers her toward the sky
Away from a land too broken
To care or understand
That she was the one
It could've loved
Protected
Not rejected solid life
Nor cooked down what she
Was meant to be
Likening her legacy
To wilted greens
Down a drain, never to be redeemed
Daughter, die no more
Leaving me to keep her name on my pen
In my fingertips
A daughter I never knew
Because they sent word by vile loathsome lips
That the bullet that tore through her live
body unjustified
Ripped the light from her eyes
Would not be held accountable
And her only justification would come
In her by and by...
Daughter, die no more
My children march on streets
Of hate
In a land that reviles and berates
Skin
And embraces
Sin
Calls Evil forth
Names it "God"
And invites it in...
No God that I know, blessed Daughter
As you will find
when you join the fold
of Real God
Divine
Daughter, die no more
die no more

Creeks
Cahooque Creek: An Ancestral Tale

Creeks hold secrets
Steeped trapped spirits
Under broken boughs
Buried vows
Along mirey floors
And holes that hold
Decaying faces
Traced in the depths
Of drowned dreams
Lost men and lost ways
Were demanded loyalty
Lost land slowly, steadily
>*Stolen in laws*
>*Diminished liberties*

Wholly counted
Halfly regarded
Men pressed
Loving women
Standing, Suffering
Holding, Bearing
Blows along shores
>*She knows more than she shows*

Creeks shudder and ripple
Filled to brims
Poisoned
Replenished
Begin again
Life teaming
Wondering when
Dark bodies bear up
From days gone

Backwater
Black waters
Stench clinging to the wind
>*Cannot wade in this water...*
>*Murky mucky water...*
>*Trying to carry fire...*
>*Mustn't lose the flame*

Creeks hold secrets
That banks remember
For now, only God can see

Deeper...Further...Back

Starting here
        going deeper
                down deeper

Past petty
        small sadness

Past last cursing
        self-cursing

Steadily looking
        Further deeper
                Lower torture

Years before
    Auto-maiming
        Mental maiming
        Lived the renamed
                formerly named
                      shame named
                            love named
                                birth named
                                      ancient names

Buried bones burrowing
        deeper in scorched earth

Back before
    Pulled bellies
        Stretching hanging
        Distorted jelly

Roads back
    Time back
        Lives back

Back before
    when simple
        never was simple

Lost time
   Long time

Dark hearts
   made darker times

Before then...
   Before then...

When was it?

What trauma-
   skinned knee
      changed us?
         Changed me?

What wordless words
   blamed me?

Why won't they
   release me?

Look further back, Woman

   Woman before...
      Woman before...
         Woman before...

Interference
   everywhere

If you want this strength

If you want this strength
Realize
That you will get this divinity

Carried and strapped in by beige,
bronzed, browned, blackened,
burnished copper arms that swung
steadily
and hands that snapped stalks, necks, peas
Fired and bubbled in anticipation
Minds that mixed ancient remedies
Voices that low uttered sounds, clicks,
chants, songs, prayers
to manifest healing
Talk the fire
Protections
Life continued
Nurtured by covered hearts that harbored
dreams
While with bent backs, they hooded eyes
and gleaned
That they might build mighty nations that
would one day overcome an interrupted
liberty

If you want this strength
Realize
That you will get this divinity

I was pushed through generations of the persistent and powerful loins of
earthbound gods who are connected to the forces greater than us all
That have poured themselves into vessels and spaces
Shifting fire, air, water, and circumstance

This clay may sometimes make me stumble
Yet greater spirits bear me up
That music in the air
Is me

If you want this strength
Realize
That you will get this divinity

This Fire Tastes Like...

This fire won't look like the last ones did
Singed souls torn up, crying, wandering,
wondering how to get love back
How to fix life
How to repair
The last fires tasted like...
Tasted like loss
Tasted like shame
Tasted like despair
Tasted like mourning
Tasted like no way out
Tasted like no way back
Tasted like Tulsa
Tasted like Elaine
Tasted like Watts
Tasted like Wilmington
Tasted like old Eppes High...
Tasted like all that it had consumed

This fire tastes different
This fire tastes fed up
This fire has eyes set
Beyond loss
Beyond prison
Beyond death
Beyond the graves
This fire has new eyes
Fixed on that "New New"
Jerusalem
New fire gonna propel these children into
promised land
They won't need the water of the oppressors
Because they are children of living waters
And raging fires
And earth that has promised fertility
Yet pushed out weeds to choke and distract

This fire tastes different
It is tastes like energy
Tastes like righteous fury
Its fuel is dark kindling root
It will combust from a place so deep
So misunderstood
So, underestimated
That it will not be contained
This fire tastes different
It tastes like resolve

It will reject any attempts to thwart combustion
The internal combustion
It will incinerate attempts at trickery for
It has seen the video and believes
It saw murderous hubris
It saw The Dead that were tried for dying
It saw the solid stance of patronizing defiance of other fires
It saw the lies stifling acrid air
This fire tastes different
It tastes alive
It will not stop until there is nothing left that can stop it
It will then scoop the ashes and build
Jerusalem
Yeah
This fire tastes different
This fire tastes like revelation
This fire tastes like change
This fire tastes like
Hope

Regina YC Garcia resides in Greenville, NC and is a Poet, Writer, Voice Artist, Narrator, and English Professor at Pitt Community College. She holds a BA in Speech Communication with a Concentration in the Oral Interpretation of Literature from The University of North Carolina at Chapel Hill, as well as a Masters in Education with a Graduate Certificate in Multicultural and Transnational Literature from East Carolina University.

She is the 2021 National DAR American Heritage Poetry Award Winner, a 2021 NCLR James Applewhite Semifinalist, and is published in a variety of journals and anthologies. Additionally, she has both written and video poetry featured in *The South Florida Poetry Journal, Up the Staircase Quarterly, The Book of Black, Black and…, The Amistad, The Black Light Project* (a documentary), and others. She additionally has upcoming work in *Main Street Rag*, and poetry and voice work to be featured in the *Sacred 9 Project*, a series of musical and literary compositions, arranged by Curtis Raybon, Director of Choirs at Tulane University.

Regina is the mother of three grown sons and one 'daughter-in-love, and is married to the wonderful Romeo A. Garcia, Jr.

Twitter: @profesoragina.com
Instagram: @profesoragina.com
Facebook: https://www.facebook.com/regina.y.garcia

www.ingramcontent.com/pod-product-compliance
Lightning Source LLC
Chambersburg PA
CBHW022125090426
42743CB00008B/1008